THE VALUE OF LEADERSHIP

The Story of Winston Churchill

VALUE COMMUNICATIONS, INC.
PUBLISHERS
SAN DIEGO, CALIFORNIA

THE VALUE OF LEADERSHIP

The Story of Winston Churchill

BY ANN DONEGAN JOHNSON

The Value of Leadership is part of the ValueTales series.

The Value of Leadership text copyright © 1987 by Ann Donegan.
Illustrations copyright © 1987 by Value Communications, Inc.
All rights reserved under International and Pan American
Copyright Conventions.

No part of this book may be reproduced in any manner
whatsoever without written permission from the publisher,
except for brief quotations embodied in reviews and articles.

First edition.
Manufactured in Canada.

For information write to : ValueTales
9601 Aero Drive, San Diego, CA 92123

ISBN 0-86679-046-2

This tale is about a great leader, Winston Churchill. The story that follows is based on events in his life. More historical facts about Winston Churchill can be found on page 63.

Once upon a time...

many years ago, a small boy named Winston Churchill sat playing with his toy soldiers. He had hundreds of them, and he loved to line them up in rows and plan make-believe battles.

Winston lived in a large, beautiful house in England with his mother and his father and his little brother, Jack. There were servants, too, to cook the meals and make the beds, to clean the house and cut the grass, and to drive the family in a horse-drawn carriage.

But even with the beautiful house and his toys and all these people around, Winston wasn't really happy. Can you guess why?

Winston was unhappy because he was lonely. His brother was still a baby and too small to play with. His parents were busy, and they spent very little time with him.

Winston's mother, Lady Randolph, was very beautiful. She loved to go to parties and dinners and visit with her friends. His father, Lord Randolph, was a politician, one of the men elected to lead the country. Lord and Lady Randolph often went out together and they traveled a great deal, but they hardly ever took Winston with them.

There was one person who did spend time with Winston, however—his nanny, Mrs. Everest. Winston called her "Woom" and he loved her dearly.

"What does my father do, Woom?" Winston asked one day.

"Your father is a leader, Winston," said Mrs. Everest.

"What does a leader do?" he asked.

"Well," she said, "a leader is someone who makes decisions for other people, someone they trust and will follow."

"I guess a leader has to be pretty wise," said Winston thoughtfully.

Being a leader sounded like an important job. Winston would have to find out more about it. Could he be a leader, too, when he grew up, he wondered.

One day when Winston was feeling even more alone than usual, something strange happened. He felt a fuzzy tickle in his ear, then a small voice whispered, "Well, Winnie, you certainly are a sad sight."

Winston looked all around. No one was there. Again the voice spoke, a bit louder this time. "I've been watching you for quite a while and you look as though you could use a friend."

Then Winston heard a soft *Poof!* and there in front of him stood a tiny golden creature. Winston was a little scared, but he tried not to show it. "Goodness!" he said. "Who are you?"

"I'm a lion of course! And quite a handsome one too, if I do say so myself. George is the name. Would you like me to be your friend?"

"Would I!" Winston beamed. He had wanted a friend for such a long time, and now, all of a sudden, he had one! But then his smile turned to a frown. "I don't think my mother would let me have a lion in the house," he said.

"Don't worry about that, Winnie," said George. "You're the only one who can see me."

Winston laughed. "That's great! We can be friends after all."

When Winston was eight years old, he was sent away to boarding school, like most children with rich and famous parents. He arrived at his new school on a dark November afternoon.

"We don't want lazy boys or day-dreamers at this school, young Winston," said the sour-looking headmaster. "We strap boys who break the rules or don't do their work. Do you understand?"

Winston was so frightened he couldn't speak.

"I said, 'Do you understand?'"

This time Winston managed to nod his head and squeak, "Yes, sir."

"Good," said the headmaster. "Now get to work."

Poor Winston. He was horribly homesick. Sitting at the back of the class the next day, he fought back the tears and thought longingly of Mrs. Everest and his toy soldiers. Suddenly he felt a tickling in his ear and a familiar voice said, "Why so downhearted, Winnie? Have you forgotten I'm here?"

Winston was overjoyed to see his friend, the little lion. "Oh, thank goodness it's you, George!" he said. "I'm in trouble already. I can do the work, but half of it doesn't make sense. And when I ask the teacher questions, he gets angry."

"There's not much you can do right now, Winnie," said George. "You will have to follow the rules. But remember that ideas can be your friends too. No matter what this teacher says or does, you can still think your own thoughts."

The months at school dragged on. Even with George there, Winston was often miserable. The teachers yelled at him and sometimes they strapped him.

On one of his visits home, Mrs. Everest noticed some bruises caused by the strap. "Why, Winston, whatever has happened to you?" she cried.

Slowly, with tears in his eyes, he told her about the school.

"My poor little boy!" Mrs. Everest gathered Winston into her arms and hugged him tightly. "This must stop right away. I'll speak to your mother and father. You won't have to go back to that school again."

Mrs. Everest kept her promise. Lord and Lady Randolph were very angry and they sent Winston to a new school. Although the teachers at this new school were much kinder, Winston still got into trouble.

"Winston, what are we going to do with you?" asked the headmaster. "Look at these notes from your teachers. *Winston is late for class. Winston does not do his homework. Winston loses his books. Winston makes no effort to improve.* I'm afraid I'm going to have to tell your parents about this."

Winston sighed. Many of the notes were true. Could such a lazy troublemaker ever grow up to be a leader?

Later when Winston was by himself, he felt the familiar tickle of George's tail in his ear.

"Hello chum. Why so glum?" George asked.

"Oh, George, I don't think I'm smart enough to be a leader."

"You're not stupid, Winston, but you are stubborn—and that gets you into trouble. Look. Do you see that tree over there? The one growing all by itself."

"Yes. What about it?"

"That tree isn't afraid to stand alone," said George. "And it's strong enough to withstand any wind. But it wasn't always, and when it was young it was smart enough to know it had to bend—or it might break."

Winston began to grin. "I think I understand. I shouldn't be afraid to stand alone either. But for now the winds are stronger than I am, so I'd better remember to bend with them."

George gave a tiny roar of approval.

Winston's father, Lord Randolph, was worried about his son. The reports from school were not good. He didn't think Winston had the ability to become a leader like himself. What job *could* Winston do when he grew up?

One time when Winston was home from school, Lord Randolph watched him playing with his toy soldiers. He had an idea. "Winston, would you like to join the army?"

Winston was delighted. "Yes, father, I'd like to very much! I'm already learning to use a rifle at school."

"Then it's settled," said his father. "Of course you will have to study very hard over the next years if you hope to get into military school."

"I will," said Winston. "I won't disappoint you."

When Winston was nearly sixteen years old, he decided he had led an army of toy soldiers long enough. On his summer holidays that year he gathered up his brother Jack, their cousins and several neighborhood children and he formed his first "real" army.

With planks and mud the boys built a fort which Winston called The Den. Inside they covered the floor with straw.

"Now as leader of this army," ordered Winston, "I want you, Jack, and the others to start digging a ditch all around The Den."

"What good will a ditch be?" asked Jack.

"We're going to fill it with water so enemy soldiers won't be able to sneak up on us," replied Winston.

"But how do we get in and out?" asked his brother.

"Why, with a drawbridge, of course!" said Winston. "We can pull the bridge up when danger approaches. And we'll build a catapult. These green apples will be great for shooting at our enemies."

"Gee!" exclaimed Jack. "You've thought of everything."

"A good leader has to be prepared," said Winston. "All right men, let's get to work!"

Back at school, Winston began to study harder. There was much to learn and he had to struggle with nearly all his subjects.

"Goodness me, you're up awfully late, Winnie," yawned a tired George one night. "It's after midnight."

"I know," said Winston. "But exams for military college are coming soon and I must pass them."

"Just do your best, Winnie. That's all anyone can do. And remember, a leader never gives up." There was a soft *Poof!* and George disappeared.

Although Winston studied very hard, he failed. He tried again, and he failed again. But Winston remembered George's advice. Finally, on his third try, he passed the exams and went to military college.

Sometimes Winston talked about his future with other students. "You know, Edward," he said one day to a friend, "I'm not going to stay in the army forever."

"Why not?" asked Edward. "It's not a bad life."

"No," replied Winston, "and there's a lot I can learn here. But what I really want to do is go into politics so I can help run the government. One day I might even be the leader of this country."

Edward laughed. "You really are a dreamer!"

Winston laughed too, but he knew it was more than just a schoolboy's dream.

Winston had loved horses all his life. Even as a little boy he'd had his own pony. So now, when he graduated from military college, he decided to join the cavalry—the part of the army that fights on horseback.

Before long his unit was sent to India. A cavalry officer's duties there were not very heavy, and Winston found himself with a lot of time on his hands.

"George," he complained one day to his little friend, "I still want to be a politician and a leader, but nothing I am doing here is helping me reach that goal."

"Then find something to do that does help," suggested George. "You know that a good leader must be able to put his ideas into words. That takes practice. And it's something you can do as easily here as at home."

"That's a terrific idea!" said Winston, and he began writing speeches and accounts of his experiences.

Winston's writing got better and better and soon newspapers were buying the things he wrote and asking him to write special articles for them.

But Winston knew he still had a lot to learn. So he asked his mother to send him books to read. He asked particularly for books about history and politics and the great leaders of the world. Nearly every letter he sent home began: "Thank you for the box of books" and ended: "Please send more."

Finally, after about three years in India, Winston decided it was time to leave the army and go home. He knew that if he couldn't get into politics right away, he could always make his living by writing.

When Winston returned to England, a newspaper asked him if he would travel to South Africa. War had broken out there between the British and the Dutch-speaking settlers called Boers, and the newspaper wanted Winston to go write about it. Winston was excited by this chance for adventure.

George liked adventure, too, but he was puzzled. "How will this trip help you become a politician?" he asked.

"Simple," said Winston. "People vote for heroes. This may be my chance to become famous."

Soon after Winston arrived in South Africa, he found himself on a train loaded with British soldiers heading for the battle zone. On the journey the train was attacked by Boers. Several railway cars bounced off the track, blocking the line. Boer soldiers seemed to be everywhere, firing steadily at the crippled train. The British fired back, but they were trapped.

Winston suddenly jumped up. "You men over there," he shouted, "follow me!"

The men obeyed. "What do you want us to do?" one asked.

"While the others are fighting, we're going to clear the track," said Winston. "It's our only hope of escape."

With bullets flying all around, it was a very dangerous task to undertake. Nonetheless, the men followed where Winston led, and soon they had the track clear. "Now we must get the wounded onto the train," ordered Winston. Just as they helped the last ones on, the Boers made a fierce attack. The train and its passengers escaped, but Winston and several British soldiers were captured and put in prison.

Winston hated prison. He asked the Boers to let him go. "I'm a writer, not a soldier," he said. They paid no attention.

So Winston decided to escape with two other prisoners. Day after day, they studied the grounds and watched how the guards went about their duties. "That guard over there often turns his back for two or three minutes at a time," observed Winston at last. "And there's a shack near the wall we could hide behind until he does."

"Then we can be over in seconds," agreed one of the others. "When shall we make our move?"

"Why wait now that we have a plan?" said Winston. "We'll go tonight."

Winston scrambled over the wall first. But before the others could join him, the guard turned back and they couldn't escape.

Winston ran and stumbled through the darkness. He jumped aboard a train that took him far from the prison. When the train stopped, he searched for a place to hide.

He was very lucky. In a country full of Boers, he found another Englishman. This man hid Winston in a coal mine for three days, then smuggled him onto another train that carried him to safety.

Hiding among the bales of wool on the train, Winston felt a tickle in his ear. "Well, well, Winnie," said George. "This adventure should make you famous and show people you have the kind of boldness a leader needs."

Winston smiled at his friend. "I sure hope you're right, George."

Winston received a hero's welcome when he returned to England. The people now knew that he was a brave man and a good leader. Winston won easily in the next election and became a member of Parliament.

"What do you plan to do now that you're in politics, Winston?" asked another politician.

"I want to help people," said Winston. "There are many who are poor and hungry. We should be doing more for them."

"That won't be an easy job," said the man.

"I'm not afraid of hard work," said Winston.

Winston loved being a politician, and he worked hard to be a good leader. He also found time to enjoy himself. One evening at a dinner party, he met Clementine Hozier.

Winston had had girl friends before, but he had never met anyone like Clementine. Not only was she beautiful, she was smart as well. And she was very interested in Winston's work.

"I'd like to see you again," said Winston. "Can I visit you soon?"

"I'd like that very much," she said. "And please call me Clemmie, all my friends do."

Winston and Clemmie began spending more and more time together. A few months later, they were married.

After they were married, Winston continued his work as a politician. He was interested in other countries and kept a close watch on their leaders. Germany worried him. He believed that country was preparing for war.

Winston went to see the Prime Minister of England to discuss his worries. "Our country is only as strong as her navy, and it needs a lot of building up."

The Prime Minister thought it over. "You might be right about the Germans," he said. "I'll put you in charge of making sure our navy is ready."

Winston began his new job as First Lord of the Admiralty right away. "This is the chance I've been waiting for," he said to George. "We need modern ships and well-trained sailors. And the old men who run the navy must be replaced."

"Hmmm," said George. "You have some good ideas, Winnie. But be careful how you treat these men. They are very powerful. Don't let them become your enemies."

"I'm not worried," he said. "What could they do to me?"

George frowned. Winston still had a few things to learn about being a leader.

Winston had been right. Germany did declare war. But thanks to Winston's leadership, the navy was ready to fight. Winston and the other politicians now spent long hours every day planning how to fight the war.

"I believe we should send battleships and soldiers to capture Turkey," said Winston. "Then we can invade Germany."

"It's not a bad idea," said one politician. "But I don't think we need as many soldiers as you say."

"And I don't think we need so many ships," said another.

Winston's idea was a good one, but the other politicians argued about how to carry it out. Months slipped by and the plans kept changing. Finally England attacked.

The attack failed. Several powerful men who didn't like Winston managed to put all the blame on him and to get him removed as leader of the navy. George had warned him about this, but Winston hadn't listened. Now he felt sad and alone.

"Oh, Clemmie, what will I do?" Winston asked his wife. "I've lost the power I worked so hard to get. I'm finished. I'm a failure."

Clemmie gave Winston a hug. "You're not a failure, dear. You made a mistake. Remember, a good leader never makes the same mistake twice. Next time try to get these people to work with you, not against you."

Even though he had lost most of his power, Winston still wanted to help England win the war. He joined the army and went to fight in France. While many soldiers were wounded or killed, Winston escaped uninjured.

"Sometimes I get the strangest feeling, George," Winston said one day. "I feel as if I'm being saved for something, as though I have an important job to do. Do you think I might still be a great leader someday?"

George twitched his tail and tickled Winston's ear. "I wouldn't be surprised at all."

After the war, Winston continued his political career, but it did not always go smoothly. Several times he quarrelled with powerful colleagues. "I tried to work with them this time, Clemmie," he explained on one such occasion. "But I'm sure what they are doing is wrong. I can't go along with it."

"Well, of course you can't. A leader has to stand up for what he thinks is right," Clemmie answered. Then she added, "Don't worry dear, your chance will come again. You must be patient, like that tree over there. Think how many winters it has waited through so it could bloom again in the spring."

Winston grinned. "Someone else once advised me to take a lesson from a tree. He was right; maybe you are too."

Over the coming years, Winston spent most of his time reading, writing articles and books about history and politics, and giving speeches.

People all over England—and in other countries as well—read what he wrote and went to hear him talk.

During these years Winston also enjoyed many happy, peaceful hours with Clemmie and their children Diana, Randolph, Sarah and Mary at Chartwell, their country home.

Winston rode his horse, painted bright pictures of the countryside and built pools for the goldfish to swim in. He even became an expert bricklayer, building his own garden walls, a couple of cottages and a brick playhouse for Mary.

Although Winston did not have much power at this time, he was still a member of Parliament, and he was deeply concerned about political events in England and other countries. Once again he watched as Germany trained soldiers and built bombs.

"Germany is preparing for war," he warned the leaders of England. "We must be prepared too. This time a strong navy won't save us. We need pilots and airplanes to protect this land."

But the leaders did not listen. Some called him an old fool. Others said he was just stirring up trouble.

Winston was old, but he was not a fool. And he wasn't the one stirring up trouble. Germany took over one of its neighbors, then another and another. World War II had begun.

"You were right, Winston," said the Prime Minister of England. "We should have listened to you. I hope it's not too late. Will you take back your old job as First Lord of the Admiralty? We need someone like you to lead our ships into battle."

Winston was very pleased to be a leader again. "Yes, sir! I'll start right away." He said a quick goodbye and rushed out the door.

During the first months of the war, it became clear that the Prime Minister was not the strong leader England needed. Neither the people nor the politicians believed in him anymore. They did believe in Winston, however.

One day the King of England called Winston to the palace. "We are facing a dark and dangerous time, Winston," he said. "We need a wise man to lead us. Will you be the new Prime Minister?"

Winston said, "Yes!" He knew he could do the job. "Thank you for this great honor, Your Majesty. I will do my best to lead our country safely through this war."

It was after midnight when Winston returned home. Everyone else in the house was asleep. He tiptoed softly into his room. George was waiting for him.

"Well, Winnie," whispered the little lion, "how was your meeting with the King?"

"It went very well, my furry friend. I'm so relieved. Now I have the power to give directions to the whole country. It's strange too. I feel as if I've been preparing for this job all my life."

George nodded—then yawned. "Right," said Winston. "It's time for bed. We should sleep now for we may not get much rest in the days ahead."

Only a few years earlier, Winston had stood before the country's politicians and warned them about the coming war. Then they had booed and hissed and called him names. Now they cheered and clapped for their new leader. They were sure that if anyone could save England, it was Winston.

He didn't make them promises he couldn't keep. He knew the war would be long and the people would face great danger. "I have nothing to offer," he said, "but blood, toil, tears and sweat."

England was not ready for war. She needed ships, planes, tanks, bullets and bombs. It would take time to build these. She needed them *now*. What could she do?

Winston and Franklin Roosevelt, the President of the United States, had been writing to each other since the start of the war. Winston decided to ask the American President for help, even though the United States was not yet in the war.

President Roosevelt sent as many supplies as he could.

The German army began its march across France. It looked as though thousands of British, French and Belgian soldiers would be captured or killed. Winston could not let that happen. He sent a rag-tag fleet of small boats, warships, freighters, sailboats—anything that would float—across the English Channel, to Dunkirk, to rescue the soldiers.

"It's taken nearly ten days, Clemmie," he said afterwards, "but we've rescued far more men than anyone thought we could. I think everyone who has a boat answered our call."

"You believed in your idea, dear," said his wife, "and you made others believe in it, too. Those soldiers who escaped will be very thankful that you didn't give up."

Winston fought the war with words as well as with ships and planes and guns. Time after time when it seemed too hard to carry on, his speeches cheered the people and gave them hope.

"We shall defend our Island whatever the cost may be," he said. "We shall fight on the beaches, we shall fight on the landing-grounds, we shall fight in the fields and in the streets. We shall fight in the hills. We shall never give up."

Now the German air force attacked England and the Battle of Britain began.

Day after day, pilots of Britain's Royal Air Force flew their planes into battle in the skies over England. The Germans had more planes and more pilots, but the Royal Air Force kept fighting.

Winston could not praise these brave men enough. He knew that these few hundred pilots were all that kept the rest of Britain safe.

"Never in the field of human conflict," he said, "was so much owed by so many to so few."

When the daytime attacks failed, the Germans tried a new plan. They began bombing London at night. The city was blacked out. No lights were allowed to shine outside to make an easy target for the German pilots.

Sometimes Winston and Clemmie would watch the night skies together, peering into the darkness that covered London like a blanket.

Suddenly the whine of the air-raid sirens filled the night. Off in the distance they could see the first bombs exploding.

"We'd better go down to the bomb shelter, Clemmie," said Winston. "I guess there'll be no sleep for us again tonight."

These nightly bombing raids continued for weeks. Many people left London. Those who couldn't leave sent their children to the country to escape the danger.

How much longer could the city last?

The people of London did not give up. Despite the bombs, the city survived. Winston often walked through the streets looking at the damage. Sometimes he walked about even as the bombs fell. He toured the airports and the shipyards. Everywhere he went, he spoke to the people, giving them the courage to fight on.

Not everyone was as brave as Winston, however. "Prime Minister, the Germans are getting closer every day," said one of his assistants. "We think the King and his family should be sent to a safer country. Perhaps the government should escape, too, while there is still time."

Winston turned and glared at the man. "Never!" he growled. "We won't run away. We will stay and fight. And we will win!"

Although Winston refused to leave England, he did agree to move his office underground. It was safer there and the bombs could do little damage.

A microphone was set up there, so Winston could speak to the English people by radio. Even when it seemed as if England might lose the war, Winston still believed they could win. When someone asked him what he would do if England ran out of weapons, he replied, "We'll hit them over the head with broomsticks if we have to!"

Slowly the power was shifting. The United States and Russia joined forces with Great Britain. Each day now brought new hope.

Although he was nearly 70 years old, Winston worked longer and harder than men half his age.

His doctor worried about his health. "You're not a young man," he scolded one day when he was called because Winston was sick. "You've already had a heart attack and pneumonia. Now you're sick again. You must take a long rest."

But Winston refused. "I'll be better soon, you'll see. I can't afford to lie in bed while there is a war to be won!"

A few days later, Winston's doctor was surprised to find his patient well again and back at work leading the country.

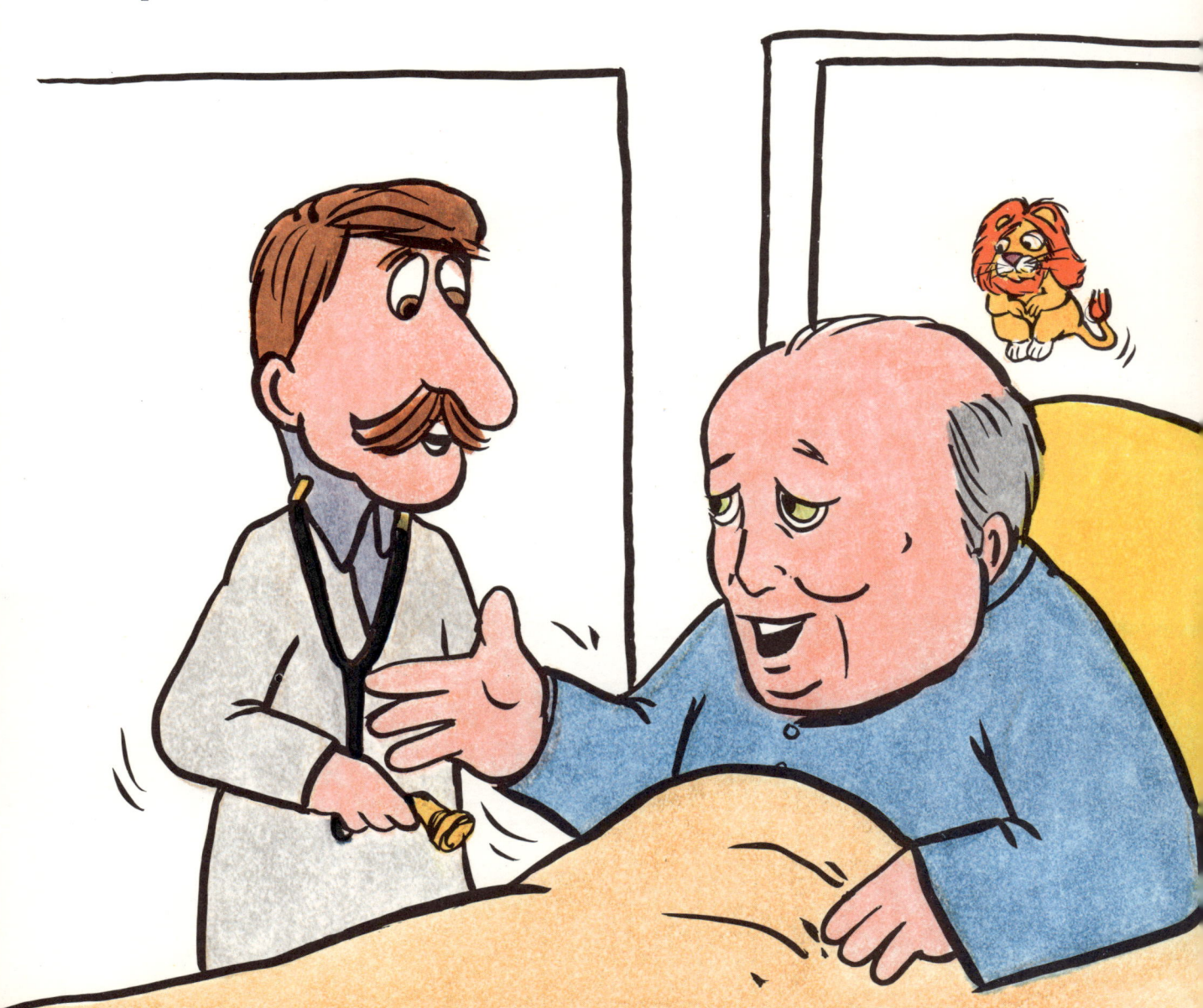

The war had been going on for more than four years. In the beginning, everything had seemed to favor Germany. That was no longer true. Once Russia and the United States had joined with Great Britain, the tide had turned. Now victory was in sight.

Winston met with Franklin Roosevelt, the President of the United States, and Josef Stalin, the Premier of Russia.

These men were the most powerful leaders in the world. They came together to talk about how to end the war and to plan the future of Europe.

At last, the great day came. After nearly six years of fighting, the war ended. When the news was announced, thousands of people ran into the streets laughing and shouting. Soldiers would be coming home soon and families could start their lives again.

As Winston stood on his balcony waving to the happy crowds, he felt a familiar tickle in his ear, like the twitching of a tiny tail.

"Hello, George!" said Winston. "Isn't this an exciting moment? I'm glad you're here to share it with me."

"You did a great job, Winnie!" said the little lion. "Who knows what might have happened if you had not been here to lead us."

The crowds cheered even louder. George gave a tiny roar of joy. Winston smiled and continued to wave to the people.

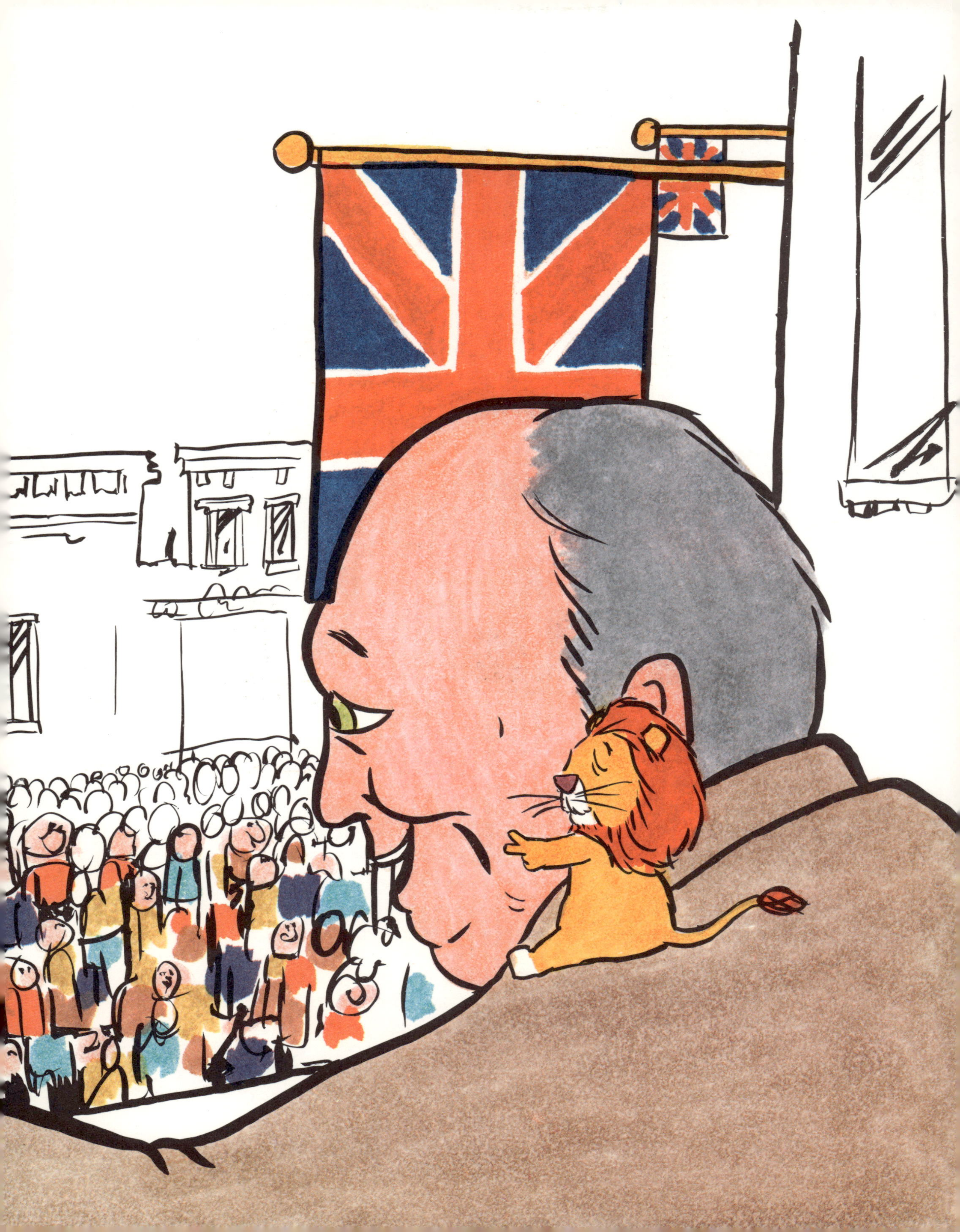

The people were thankful for Winston's leadership during World War II, but once the fighting was over they wanted a change. They voted for someone else as Prime Minister of England. Winston lost his job. He was heart-broken, because he wanted to continue his work for world peace.

Winston and Clemmie moved back to Chartwell, their country home. He began painting again and he continued to write books. He rode his horse and he played with his grandchildren.

Several years later, when Winston was almost 77, another election was held. Once more, he was chosen as Prime Minister, the most important leader in Great Britain.

In the coming years, Winston received many awards. The Queen of England made him a knight. From then on he was called *Sir* Winston Churchill. He also received another great honor, a Nobel prize for his writing and his speeches.

On his eightieth birthday, hundreds of people around the world sent him cards and presents. They wanted to thank him for his great leadership, especially during World War II.

Winston was delighted. "You've made me very happy," he said. "But it was you people who had the lion's heart and the lion's courage. I was just called on to give the lion's roar."

Winston Churchill was a special person. He became one of the greatest leaders in the world.

You are special too. There's no one else exactly like you. Winston had a dream. He wanted to be a great leader. What is your dream?

No matter what you want to be, you'll find the road to your dream easier if you follow Winston Churchill's example. Work hard, learn from your mistakes and believe in yourself. If you do that, you'll lead a happier and more rewarding life.

The End

Historical Facts

Statesman, soldier, author and artist, Winston Churchill was involved in every important event in his country's history from the Boer War (1899–1902) through World War II (1939–1945).

He was born on November 30, 1874, at Blenheim Palace in Oxfordshire, England. His family was both wealthy and famous. One of his ancestors, John Churchill, Duke of Marlborough, had been a great military hero. Blenheim Palace was built in the early 1700s to reward Marlborough for his victories. Winston's father, Lord Randolph Churchill, was a well-known Conservative politician, and his mother was a very beautiful American, Jennie Jerome.

As a youngster, Winston Churchill showed no signs of potential greatness. He was an unhappy and neglected child. Only his nurse, Mrs. Everest, paid much attention to him. He was troublesome at school, and during the four years he attended Harrow, one of England's best schools, he was a poor student. However, he was fascinated by military subjects and decided to go into the army. He had to write his exams three times before he finally passed and was able to go to the Royal Military Academy at Sandhurst. He did very well there, and after he graduated he joined the British Army in 1895.

While he was in the army, he served in Cuba, India and the Sudan in Africa. In his spare time, he began to read very extensively and to write. He wrote three books and sold many articles to British newspapers.

In 1899, Churchill left the army to run for Parliament but was defeated. He went instead to South Africa as a newspaper reporter to cover the Boer War. Although he was not there as a soldier, he involved himself in the fighting and was captured by the Boers. After a month in prison, he made a daring escape, crossing hundreds of miles of enemy territory to reach safety. This exploit was widely reported in British newspapers and Churchill was greeted as a hero when he returned to England. He ran again for Parliament in 1900 and won.

In 1904, Churchill disagreed with his party, the Conservatives, over trade policy and joined the Liberal government. He held a variety of posts in the government and in 1911 became First Lord of the Admiralty, the minister responsible for the Royal Navy. He was very concerned about the possibility of war with Germany, and worked to make sure that the navy was ready to fight when World War I did break out in 1914. However, his success at the Admiralty did not last. He masterminded a plan to capture the Turkish peninsula of Gallipoli, but the plan was badly carried out and many British soldiers were killed. Churchill was forced to resign from the government. He returned to the army and fought for a year in France.

In 1916, Churchill returned to Parliament and in 1924 he rejoined the Conservative Party. He did not, however, achieve much political success again until 1939. Although he was still a member of Parliament, he had almost no power or influence. He spent much of his

WINSTON SPENCER CHURCHILL
1874–1965

time at his country house, Chartwell, with his wife Clementine, whom he had married in 1908, and their four children. He busied himself with various hobbies, particularly painting, and made his living by writing.

As the 1930s went on, Churchill became more and more alarmed by the threat of another war with Germany. Again and again he warned politicians and the British people against Nazi Germany. He disagreed with his own party, led by Prime Minister Neville Chamberlain, because they were trying to keep the peace by agreeing to Hitler's demands. When Germany invaded Poland in 1939, Britons realized that Chamberlain's policy of appeasement had been wrong and that Churchill had been right about Germany's aggressive intentions. In 1940 Chamberlain was forced to resign and Churchill became prime minister.

Throughout the war, Churchill inspired the British people to courage, hope and endurance. His speeches and radio broadcasts were very effective in keeping up the nation's morale. Again and again, he insisted that Britain would never surrender and that it would eventually win the war. He himself seemed fearless. He made a point of being seen in the bomb-damaged streets of London, defiantly raising his hand in the famous "V" for Victory sign. He became the living symbol of Britain's determination to win the war.

Nonetheless, once the war was won, Britain was ready for a change of government. The Conservatives led by Churchill were defeated, and the Labour Party took over. Churchill continued to be active politically in other ways. He spoke out against the Soviet Union, and was the first to use the term "Iron Curtain" to describe the division of Europe after the war. He also continued to write, including two of his best known series, *The Second World War* and *A History of the English-Speaking Peoples*.

In 1951, when he was 77, Churchill again became prime minister. He remained in office until 1955. By this time, he was beloved and admired as a strong and heroic leader of his people, especially because of his leadership during the difficult years of World War II. He was honored in many ways during these years. In 1953, he was knighted and in the same year he also received the Nobel Prize for Literature. In 1963 he was made an honorary citizen of the United States.

Winston Churchill died on January 24, 1965, at the age of 90, and was given a state funeral at which people from all over the world came to pay him tribute.

The ValueTale Series

THE VALUE OF BELIEVING IN YOURSELF	The Story of Louis Pasteur
THE VALUE OF DETERMINATION	The Story of Helen Keller
THE VALUE OF PATIENCE	The Story of the Wright Brothers
THE VALUE OF KINDNESS	The Story of Elizabeth Fry
THE VALUE OF HUMOR	The Story of Will Rogers
THE VALUE OF TRUTH AND TRUST	The Story of Cochise
THE VALUE OF CARING	The Story of Eleanor Roosevelt
THE VALUE OF COURAGE	The Story of Jackie Robinson
THE VALUE OF CURIOSITY	The Story of Christopher Columbus
THE VALUE OF RESPECT	The Story of Abraham Lincoln
THE VALUE OF IMAGINATION	The Story of Charles Dickens
THE VALUE OF FAIRNESS	The Story of Nellie Bly
THE VALUE OF SAVING	The Story of Benjamin Franklin
THE VALUE OF LEARNING	The Story of Marie Curie
THE VALUE OF SHARING	The Story of the Mayo Brothers
THE VALUE OF RESPONSIBILITY	The Story of Ralph Bunche
THE VALUE OF HONESTY	The Story of Confucius
THE VALUE OF GIVING	The Story of Ludwig van Beethoven
THE VALUE OF UNDERSTANDING	The Story of Margaret Mead
THE VALUE OF LOVE	The Story of Johnny Appleseed
THE VALUE OF FORESIGHT	The Story of Thomas Jefferson
THE VALUE OF HELPING	The Story of Harriet Tubman
THE VALUE OF DEDICATION	The Story of Albert Schweitzer
THE VALUE OF FRIENDSHIP	The Story of Jane Addams
THE VALUE OF FANTASY	The Story of Hans Christian Andersen
THE VALUE OF ADVENTURE	The Story of Sacagawea
THE VALUE OF CREATIVITY	The Story of Thomas Edison
THE VALUE OF FACING A CHALLENGE	The Story of Terry Fox
THE VALUE OF CHARITY	The Story of Cardinal Léger
THE VALUE OF TENACITY	The Story of Maurice Richard
THE VALUE OF DISCIPLINE	The Story of Alexander Graham Bell
THE VALUE OF BOLDNESS	The Story of Captain James Cook
THE VALUE OF COMPASSION	The Story of Florence Nightingale
THE VALUE OF LEADERSHIP	The Story of Winston Churchill

Value Tales™